SANTA CRUZ KINDERGARTEN

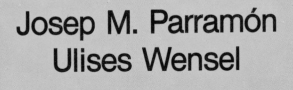

Josep M. Parramón
Ulises Wensel

Autumn

Belair
PUBLISHING COMPANY INC.

SANTA CRUZ KINDERGARTEN

Summer color,

Autumn color

Green, brown, red, gold,
tan, yellow...

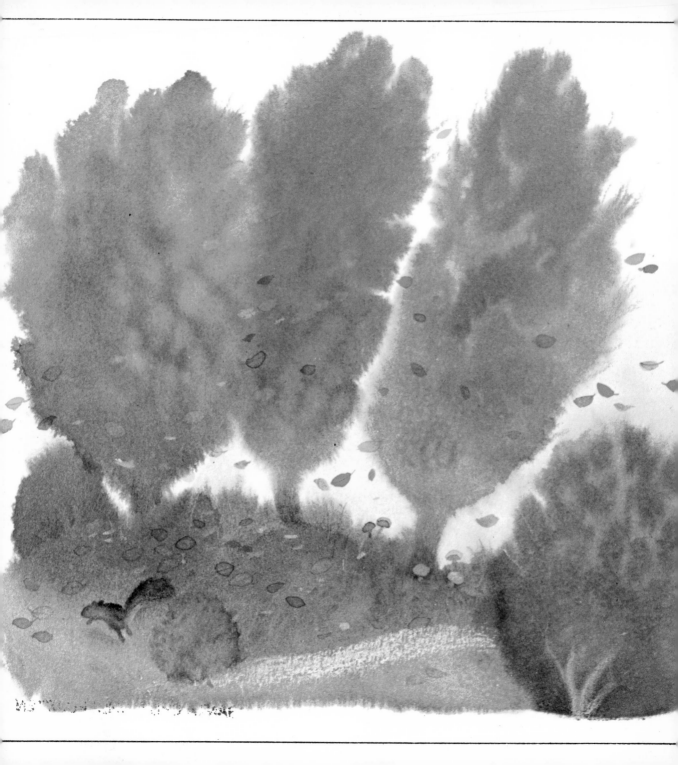

Leaves fall

Wonderful Autumn!

So long, vacation!

Back to the city

Back to school

Back to books

Night comes earlier...

The rains begin

It is the season
for making ~~wine~~
cider.

The season for canning

It's autumn!

AUTUMN

Change of season; change of colors.

No season is like autumn. In no other season does nature have such a marvelous change of color. From all shades of green in July and August nature changes to brown, red, tan, gold and yellow in October. Wonderful autumn!

The wind is chilly; it rains; the birds fly south.

The weather is unsettled now. The winds become colder as we move into autumn and chilly rains fall. The birds fly south. They flew north in the spring, built their nests and laid their eggs. And now that it is autumn, the whole family flies south.

It is the season for hunting.

In the countryside, this is the season for hunting. The hunters take their rifles and look for rabbits, pheasants, ducks, deer, and quail.

Life begins again in the field.

When autumn comes, the farmer plows the field and leaves it in rows to make the soil loose and let the air enter it. When spring comes the farmer will plant seeds in the soil.

Autumn begins on the 21st of September and ends on the 21st of December.